Library of
Davidson College

The Artificial Jungle

A SUSPENSE THRILLER

by *CHARLES LUDLAM*

No part of this book may be reproduced, stored in a retrieval system, or transmitted in any form, by any means, including mechanical, electronic, photocopying, recording, or otherwise, without the prior written permission of the publisher.

SAMUEL FRENCH, INC.
45 WEST 25TH STREET   NEW YORK 10010
7623 SUNSET BOULEVARD   HOLLYWOOD 90046
LONDON   *TORONTO*

Copyright ©, 1986, by Charles Ludlam
Copyright ©, 1987, by The Estate of Charles Ludlam

ALL RIGHTS RESERVED

CAUTION: Professionals and amateurs are hereby warned that THE ARTIFICIAL JUNGLE is subject to a royalty. It is fully protected under the copyright laws of the United States of America, the British Commonwealth, including Canada, and all other countries of the Copyright Union. All rights, including professional, amateur, motion pictures, recitation, lecturing, public reading, radio broadcasting, television, and the rights of translation into foreign languages are strictly reserved. In its present form the play is dedicated to the reading public only.

THE ARTIFICIAL JUNGLE may be given stage presentation by amateurs upon payment of a royalty of Sixty Dollars for the first performance, and Forty Dollars for each additional performance, payable one week before the date when the play is given to Samuel French, Inc., at 45 West 25th Street, New York, N.Y. 10010, or at 7623 Sunset Boulevard, Hollywood, Calif. 90046, or to Samuel French (Canada), Ltd., 80 Richmond Street East, Toronto, Ontario, Canada M5C 1P1.

Royalty of the required amount must be paid whether the play is presented for charity or gain and whether or not admission is charged.

Stock royalty quoted on application to Samuel French, Inc.

For all other rights than those stipulated above, apply to Samuel French, Inc. 45 West 25th Street, New York, N.Y. 10010.

Particular emphasis is laid on the question of amateur or professional readings, permission and terms for which must be secured in writing from Samuel French, Inc.

Copying from this book in whole or in part is strictly forbidden by law, and the right of performance is not transferable.

Whenever the play is produced the following notice must appear on all programs, printing and advertising for the play: "Produced by special arrangement with Samuel French, Inc."

Due authorship credit must be given on all programs, printing and advertising for the play.

> Anyone presenting the play shall not commit or authorize any act or omission by which the copyright of the play or the right to copyright same may be impaired.

> No changes shall be made in the play for the purpose of your production unless authorized in writing.

> The publication of this play does not imply that it is necessarily available for performance by amateurs or professionals. Amateurs and professionals considering a production are strongly advised in their own interests to apply to Samuel French, Inc., for consent before starting rehearsals, advertising, or booking a theatre or hall.

Printed in U.S.A.
ISBN 0-573-69072-3

> **BILLING AND CREDIT REQUIREMENTS**
> All producers of THE ARTIFICIAL JUNGLE must give credit to the Author in all programs and in all instances in which the title of the Play appears for purposes of advertising, publicizing or otherwise exploiting the Play and/or production. The author's name must appear on a separate line in which no other name appears, immediately following the title of the play, and must appear in size of type not less than fifty percent the size of title type.

in

THE ARTIFICIAL JUNGLE

A Suspense Thriller

Written and Directed by
CHARLES LUDLAM

Starring

CHARLES LUDLAM	**EVERETT QUINTON**
BLACK-EYED SUSAN	**PHILIP CAMPANARO**

ETHYL EICHELBERGER

Set by	*Costumes by*	*Lights by*
JACK KELLY	**EVERETT QUINTON**	**RICHARD CURRIE**

Original Music Composed by
PETER GOLUB

CAST

Frankie Spinelli .... PHILIP CAMPANARO

Chester Nurdiger .... CHARLES LUDLAM

Roxanne Nurdiger .... BLACK-EYED SUSAN

Mrs. Nurdiger .... ETHYL EICHELBERGER

Zachary Slade .... EVERETT QUINTON

966 Rivington Street in lower Manhattan.

THERE WILL BE A FIFTEEN-MINUTE INTERMISSION AFTER ACT I.

CAST OF CHARACTERS

ROXANNE NURDIGER — Roxy for short.
CHESTER NURDIGER — her husband, a loveable sap.
MRS. NURDIGER — her mother-in-law.
ZACHARY SLADE — a drifter and a smoothie.
FRANKIE SPINELLI — a cop, somebody's brother-in-law.

The scene is set in a pet shop on Manhattan's Lower East Side. It is not a well kept shop. But rather a family affair with the owners living in the back of the store. Stacked bird cages, bubbling aquariums and rodent cages create an atmosphere of general disorder. Large potted plants and lush foliage lend a tropical touch. The overall effect is one of denseness and kitsch exoticism. It is clear that these people are creatures of fantasy. Fishnets, and other jungle and sea motifs are overlaid with five-and-ten-cent store modern furniture. We sit in the back of the store and look out through the shop to the street where occasional passers-by stop and look in the window. Signs naming species and prices break up the otherwise tropical effect. A sign on the window spells Pet Shop backwards.

The Artificial Jungle

ACT ONE

FRANKIE. That bird you sold me just won't talk.
CHESTER. It talked here. You heard it.
FRANKIE. Yeah, but it hasn't said a word since I got it home.
CHESTER. Give it time. Give it time.
FRANKIE. I've had it three weeks. And the damn bird doesn't say anything. It just sits there.
CHESTER. Sometimes they have to get used to the new environment.
FRANKIE. I guess. The kids are real disappointed. They keep asking me — when's the birdie gonna talk, daddy? when's the birdie gonna talk? I feel like an asshole.
CHESTER. You better watch your language around it. You know the story of the old lady and the parrot. They pick up profanity.
FRANKIE. This one ain't pickin' up anything. It's just a dumb bird.
CHESTER. Well, it was talking here. Be patient. When the time comes it will talk.
FRANKIE. I hope so. I hate to think I wasted my money.
CHESTER. Maybe what you need is a train-your-bird-to-talk record.
FRANKIE. No.
CHESTER. Here, look at this. "Your bird, too, can be a star." Now, this side teaches it to say "Hello" and "Pretty Boy."

FRANKIE. What's on the other side?
CHESTER. "Polly Want a Cracker." Now that's a parrot classic! I'll tell you what—it's four ninety-eight, I'll give you a break on it. Four eighty-nine.
FRANKIE. You're a real sport.
CHESTER. You need any birdseed, anything like that?
FRANKIE. A small bag.
CHESTER. One small bag coming up. (*Places huge bag on counter.*) You know, maybe your bird needs a more balanced diet. Have you thought of getting it some pro-so millet?
FRANKIE. No.
CHESTER. Sometimes this will get them talking right away.
FRANKIE. Well, try it.
CHESTER. Or maybe your bird is bored.
FRANKIE. Now that's a possibility.
CHESTER. We have a whole line of bird toys and amusements here. We've got a bird ferris wheel. We got a bird mirror—he could admire himself. We got a bird dumbbell—he could pump up. And we got a bird—we got a bird—pipe. Now what the hell is that? (*Tosses it back.*) Do you have *Parrots of the World*?
FRANKIE. No.
CHESTER. Look at this. Over one hundred full-color photographs of every parrot known to man. Oh, look at that one!
FRANKIE. Oh, that looks like Tweetheart!
CHESTER. Yeah, that looks like yours, doesn't it? I think you should get that for the kids. It's very educational.
FRANKIE. Well, you might as well throw that in too.
CHESTER. Throw that in. So, Frankie. Anything else I can get you?

THE ARTIFICIAL JUNGLE

FRANKIE. How about something in the way of a birdbath?

CHESTER. One birdbath coming up. (*It's a dog dish.*) Let me add this up for you.

MRS. NURDIGER. (*off*) Roxanne, did you clean the gerbils' cages?

ROXANNE. Yes.

MRS. NURDICER. (*off*) Did you feed the piranhas?

ROXANNE. (*entering*) I'm doing it now.

FRANKIE. Hi, Roxanne.

ROXANNE. Aw hi yourself.

FRANKIE. Whatsamatter with her?

CHESTER. Oh she's got the rag on.

ROXANNE. Fuck off.

CHESTER. Nice talk.

ROXANNE. Oh, leave me alone, will ya? I'm in no mood.

FRANKIE. She's been like this for weeks.

CHESTER. I don't know what's eating her. Women, you can't figure 'em. (*Calculates on the back of a brown paper sack.*) That'll be forty-nine dollars and ninety-eight cents — eighty-nine cents. I'm giving you a break on the record. Oh She's going to feed the piranhas. Don't miss this.

(*ROXANNE lowers slab of meat into piranha tank, removes bloody bone and disposes of it in kitchen.*)

CHESTER. My they were hungry.

FRANKIE. Maybe she's bored. Everybody needs a vacation once in a while.

CHESTER. Naw. I took her to the tropical fish show in Pittsburgh. And even that didn't snap her out of it.

ROXANNE. (*looking at cages*) Ooooh, the rats had another litter.

FRANKIE. Maybe it's time you two thought about raising a family.

CHESTER. Look, we got baby rats. What do we need children for?

ROXANNE. Ooh wittle baby wats. Hewo babies. Hewo.

FRANKIE. (*They both look over at ROXANNE.*) Think about it.

CHESTER. Yeah, yeah, I'll think about it.

FRANKIE. I gotta go.

CHESTER. You gonna play dominoes tonight?

FRANKIE. What is tonight?

CHESTER. Thursday.

FRANKIE. Right. I'll be here. Wednesday bowling, Thursday dominoes.

CHESTER. We're gonna be playing for blood tonight, baby.

FRANKIE. See you later.

CHESTER. See you later. Oh, Frankie, don't forget your change. (*Hands him a pittance.*)

FRANKIE. See you later Roxanne.

ROXANNE. Not if I see you first.

(*FRANKIE exits.*)

ROXANNE. How could you have sold him that bird? You know it doesn't talk.

CHESTER. I didn't want to sell it to him. He insisted on buying it.

ROXANNE. It was a dirty trick to play on a pal.

CHESTER. I was trying to put one over on this rich dame. You know, making the bird talk by ventriloquism. Suddenly he came into the shop. I'm just about to clinch the deal when he horns in and says he wants to buy

THE ARTIFICIAL JUNGLE 11

the bird for his kids. The rich dame bowed out. What could I do but sell it to him?

ROXANNE. You could have told him the truth.

CHESTER. Are you kidding? He's a cop. He'd probably arrest me.

ROXANNE. You're his best friend.

CHESTER. Listen, he's got more morals than he knows what to do with. He'd arrest his own mother for jay walking. I didn't have the heart to tell him. It would ruin a beautiful friendship.

ROXANNE. Then take the bird back and give him a refund.

CHESTER. I hate to do it. It's not so much the bird as the money has sentimental value to me.

ROXANNE. Chester, you're going to take that bird back and give him a refund. Because if you don't I will.

CHESTER. Alright, alright. Give it a few more days. The bird might talk, you never know.

MRS. NURDIGER. (*calling from off*) Roxanne, two portions of tubifex worms.

ROXANNE. Coming up! (*sighs*)

CHESTER. Whatsamatter?

ROXANNE. Nothing.

CHESTER. It's something. You're not your old self. You walk around here mopin' and sighin'.

ROXANNE. You know I'm not nuts about handling tubifex worms. They give me the creeps.

CHESTER. You're sure that's all it is?

ROXANNE. Sure.

CHESTER. Maybe you're overworked.

ROXANNE. We could use some help around here.

CHESTER. It's always been a family business. I never thought of hiring anybody from the outside.

ROXANNE. Maybe just to handle the worms, clean the

rat cages. You know — the disgusting stuff. You know I don't mind the birds and the tropical fish — they're pretty.

CHESTER. Okay. If it will make you happy, why not? Here. I'll put a sign in the window. (*Makes sign. Reads.*) "Help wanted." (*Puts sign in window.*) There. Are you satisfied?

MRS. NURDIGER. (*voice off*) Roxanne, I need two dozen mouse pinks.

ROXANNE. (*groans*) Mouse pinks! That's another thing. I just don't feature feeding baby mice to the snakes.

CHESTER. But that's what they eat.

ROXANNE. But their eyes aren't even open yet.

CHESTER. They was just born. They never know what hit 'em.

ROXANNE. It seems cruel.

CHESTER. That's the law of the jungle. Every animal preys on some other animal.

ROXANNE. What about vegetarians?

(*ZACHARY SLADE walks by shop, sees the sign and enters, unnoticed. He leafs through a book on the counter as the conversation continues.*)

CHESTER. What, you think plants have no feelings? Just because they don't scream, they don't cry out when they're hurt? Believe me they feel plenty. In fact vegetables are probably more sensitive than people.

ROXANNE. Some people.

CHESTER. Every living thing lives off some other living thing. That's the law of the jungle.

ROXANNE. But why create an artificial jungle?

THE ARTIFICIAL JUNGLE

CHESTER. It's educational and amusing. What better occupation than to study nature—its beauty and its cruelty.

ZACHARY. (*carrying the help wanted sign*) Excuse me, you're looking for help?

CHESTER. Yeah. You had any experience in the pet trade?

ZACHARY. I know tropicals.

CHESTER. Latin names?

ZACHARY. I can tell a Hyphessobrycon heterorhabdus from an astronotus ocellatus.

CHESTER. Very good, very good.

ROXANNE. What did he say?

CHESTER. He can tell an Oscar from a flag tetra.

ROXANNE. So he knows Latin. But can he change hamster cages?

ZACHARY. I've done my share of that. What's the deal?

ROXANNE. Long hours—low pay.

ZACHARY. I'll take it.

CHESTER. Well, you see, I'm seeing several other applicants. Come back tomorrow and I'll let you know.

ZACHARY. Okay. I'll come back tomorrow. (*goes out*)

MRS. NURDIGER. (*calls from off*) Roxanne, I need two portions of tubifex worms!

ROXANNE. What are you stallin' for? Call him back. Hire him.

CHESTER. I don't know anything about him. How do I know he'll work out?

ROXANNE. Try him and see, Chester. Because if you think I'm going to go on dishing up these disgusting worms you've got another thing coming, I quit!

MRS. NURDIGER. (*off*) Roxanne worms!

CHESTER. Roxanne, mother needs worms.
ROXANNE. Let her get her own worms, Chester. I'm not putting my hands in that filth again.
CHESTER. Oh alright, alright! I'll see if I can still catch him. (*runs out*)
MRS. NURDIGER. (*enters frantically*) Roxanne, I want two portions of tubifex worms and I'm tired of waiting!

(*ROXANNE sits staring straight ahead ignoring the old lady.*)

MRS. NURDIGER. Sulking again. I'll get them myself. (*Goes to refrigerator and opens dish and scoops out two dollops of worms and puts them in dixie cups which she closes.*) I do wish you'd snap out of it. (*exits*)

(*ROXANNE rises and begins prowling around the room restlessly as if she were about to explode. CHESTER reenters with ZACHARY.*)

CHESTER. Say, how old are you?
ZACHARY. Thirty-four.
CHESTER. That's a good age. I need somebody young to help me take care of my business. Young, but not a kid, if you know what I mean.
ZACHARY. Young, but not a kid. I guess that description fits me alright.
CHESTER. What's your name?
ZACHARY. Zachary, Zachary Slade. My friends call me Zack.
CHESTER. You got friends?
ZACHARY. What do you mean by that?
CHESTER. Nothing, it was just a joke. I'm Chester

THE ARTIFICIAL JUNGLE 15

Nurdiger. (*They shake hands.*) This is my wife, Roxanne. The little Nurdiger.

ZACHARY. Nice meeting you.

ROXANNE. How do you know? You haven't met me long enough to know whether it's nice or not.

CHESTER. Oh, here comes Mrs. Muncie to get the weekly rat for her boa constrictor. (*Mrs. Muncie enters.*) Hello, Mrs. Muncie.

MRS. MUNCIE. Hello, Chester.

CHESTER. We have a big fat rat for you today. (*Bags the rat.*) Ninety-eight cents . . . a dollar for you.

MRS. MUNCIE. Thank you. Give my love to your mother. (*exits*)

CHESTER. Bye, Mrs. Muncie. Great gal, Mrs. Muncie. I've got to go see my bird man, pick up a shipment of canaries. Roxanne will break you in. (*exits*)

ROXANNE. You keep reptiles?

ZACHARY. Yeah, python, couple a boas.

ROXANNE. Well, you get a discount on rats here. Sorta makes up for the low pay—if you're into reptiles.

ZACHARY. Yeah, I'm into reptiles. (*Their eyes meet. She turns away. He slips up behind her and whispers in her ear.*) Why did you marry this guy, anyway?

ROXANNE. (*turns on him as if stung*) That's none of your business.

ZACHARY. Unless I make it mine.

ROXANNE. You've got some gall.

ZACHARY. A man who never makes a pass at a woman has to settle for the women who make passes at him.

MRS. NURDIGER. (*voice off*) Roxanne, two tubifex.

ROXANNE. Get me a couple of portions of tubifex.

ZACHARY. Where are they?

ROXANNE. They're in the refrigerator—in a plastic container.

ZACHARY. (*Opens the refrigerator and screams.*)

ROXANNE. (*unruffled*) Something wrong?

ZACHARY. They moved.

ROXANNE. They should, they're alive. Or didn't you know? Say, how long have you been in the pet trade?

ZACHARY. I had a goldfish when I was a kid.

ROXANNE. You gotta be kidding! What about all those Latin names?

ZACHARY. You've got a very informative book out there on the rack and I'm a fast learner.

ROXANNE. Here, let me do that. (*She takes the tubifex to Mrs. Nurdiger.*) What makes you think I won't tell him you're a phoney?

ZACHARY. You won't. Besides, I'm not a phoney. I'm a Jack-of-all-trades.

ROXANNE. And a master of none?

ZACHARY. Maybe, but I'm sure you'll find some use for me when he's not around. I've been everything from a golf caddy to an insurance salesman. I can give a Swedish massage and instructions on the mandolin. (*Comes up behind her and takes her in his arms.*)

ROXANNE. Do you sell accident insurance?

ZACHARY. Why, is somebody going to have an accident?

ROXANNE. You never know.

ZACHARY. Don't you carry insurance?

ROXANNE. Oh yeah, public liability, collision, fire, and theft. (*dreamily*) But I was thinking more along the lines of accident insurance. Chester is accident prone.

ZACHARY. I'll talk to him about it.

ROXANNE. Does he have to know? I mean, can't I just insure him without asking?

ZACHARY. He's got to sign.

ROXANNE. I hate to alarm him.

THE ARTIFICIAL JUNGLE 17

ZACHARY. Whatsamatter? Afraid he'll find out he's worth more to you dead than alive?

(*Enter CHESTER with a crate of canaries.*)

CHESTER. What a bunch of canaries! There's not a bad singer in the lot. I'm sorry I was away so long. (*Kisses ROXANNE.*) Are you cross with me?
ROXANNE. No.
CHESTER. I tell you, Roxanne, you've never seen such carnaries, and all in perfect feather. You just want to love them to death. (*The birds sing.*) Listen, they're singing. (*Whistles along with the canaries.*) Wait till I show Mamma! (*exits*) Mamma! Mamma!
ROXANNE. I hate him.

(*CHESTER reenters with MRS. NURDIGER.*)

MRS. NURDIGER. What varieties did he have?
CHESTER. They're all American Singers.
MRS. NURDIGER. I can hear it.
CHESTER. Oh, and Mamma, this is our new employee, Mr. Zachary Slade.
MRS. NURDIGER. How do you do, Mr. Slade.
ZACHARY. My friends call me Zack.
MRS. NURDIGER. Well, perhaps someday if we become friends I'll call you that too, Mr. Slade. Have you had much experience in the pet trade?
ZACHARY. (*glances nervously at ROXANNE*) Well as a matter of fact I . . .
ROXANNE. Oh he's an expert. You don't have to worry about that.
CHESTER. That's right, Mamma. You should hear him rattle off those Latin names.

MRS. NURDIGER. Oh, I don't care about book learning. It's just that inexperienced people tend to be squeamish. Are you squeamish, Mr. Slade?

ZACHARY. Squeamish? No.

MRS. NURDIGER. Pet people have to handle a lot of things in the course of a day that would put most grown men into a dead faint. (*They all laugh— ZACK a little uneasily.*) I hope you'll like working here. We don't make much money. But we have a lot of fun.

ZACHARY. Oh, I like it alright. But I can see room for improvement.

MRS. NURDIGER. Improvement? What kind of improvement?

ZACHARY. Well, your sign, for instance. It's a wonder you do any business at all with a sign like that.

CHESTER. What's wrong with the sign?

ZACHARY. It just says Pet Shop.

CHESTER. But that's what it is—a pet shop.

ZACHARY. Sure it is. But there are a million pet shops. But what makes this pet shop different from all the others? You need something to make this shop different and you need a neon sign to say so.

MRS. NURDIGER. Neon sign?

CHESTER. What's the point? The shop isn't open at night. Neon shows up better at night.

ZACHARY. People will see it coming home from work. You could leave it on all night. Believe me it will give you presence here.

CHESTER. We've already been here for twenty-five years.

ZACHARY. All the more reason to make it new.

CHESTER. Look, I don't want us to look like one of those discount pet places. This is a family business. It has

THE ARTIFICIAL JUNGLE 19

a personal touch. I know it isn't a slick operation. It may look a little like a jungle — but I like it that way.

MRS. NURDIGER. I'm afraid we're set in our ways, Mr. Slade.

ZACHARY. I'm not saying change the character of the place. But merchandise it. You like it like a jungle — good. Make other people like it too. You have to tell them what to think. Call it The Artificial Jungle and put it up there in neon light. Advertise it on television and believe me you'll make plenty.

MRS. NURDIGER. You certainly have a lot of ideas, Mr. Slade. (*Shop bell off. — it's FRANKIE.*) There's a customer. Would you get it, Roxanne. (*ROXANNE doesn't move.*) Oh, alright, I'll go.

ZACHARY. Please, allow me.

MRS. NURDIGER. Oh, no, Mr. Slade, please don't bother. I'll take care of it.

ZACHARY. It's no bother. After all what am I here for, but to take some of the burden off of you. (*exits into shop*)

MRS. NURDIGER. What a nice young man.

ROXANNE. I don't like him.

CHESTER. Why on earth not?

ROXANNE. All he does is talk talk talk.

CHESTER. He was making a lot of sense just now.

ROXANNE. You should never have hired him.

CHESTER. You were the one who insisted.

ROXANNE. Me? Don't blame it on me.

MRS. NURDIGER. Now Roxanne, you know you've been asking for help with the dirty work. Look at the clock. It's almost closing time.

ZACHARY. (*entering*) There's a gentleman here who wants to return a parrot.

CHESTER. Return a parrot? Oh that's no gentleman that's Frankie Spinelli. Officer Spinelli, what can I do you for?

FRANKIE. (*entering*) Take back this damn bird will you, Chester.

CHESTER. I don't know, the store has a no return policy.

FRANKIE. But the damn bird won't talk.

CHESTER. It talked for me.

FRANKIE. Well, it won't talk for me.

CHESTER. How much will you pay me to take it off your hands?

FRANKIE. You know I'd almost be willing to pay you just to be rid of this lousy bird. (*Falling on his knees and pleading with mock tears.*) Chester please — please, Chester take back the bird Chester, have a heart Chester, . . . Chester . . . (*Pretends to break down.*)

CHESTER. (*playing along*) Oh alright. I really shouldn't but as a favor to a friend . . . just this once . . . I'll take it back.

FRANKIE. (*kissing his hands in mock gratitude*) Thank you! Thank you! (*Hands him the cage with the parrot.*)

PARROT. (*as soon as it is in CHESTER'S hands*) Gawk! Polly want a cracker.

FRANKIE. God damn! Did you hear that?

CHESTER. Frankie, please, your language, this bird is very impressionable.

FRANKIE. Give it here. I was wrong. I'll keep it.

CHESTER. No, Frankie, somehow I have a feeling this bird will only talk for me.

PARROT. Hiya handsome! Hiya handsome!

FRANKIE. Maybe I should take it home and give it another chance.

ROXANNE. Naw, you heard what he said, Frankie. It's a one man bird.

THE ARTIFICIAL JUNGLE

PARROT. How much are the turtles?
FRANKIE. Shut up!
PARROT. Shut up! Shut up! Shut up!
FRANKIE. I can't figure it.
CHESTER. Come on. Don't let a bird brain get you down. Let's play some serious dominoes here. Frankie, this is my new employee, Zack Slade. Zack, this is Frankie Spinelli, my cousin. Aw hell, my best friend. (*ZACK and FRANKIE shake hands.*) Frankie is one of New York's finest.
ZACHARY. You've got guts. I couldn't cut it.
FRANKIE. Sometimes you find out you've got guts you didn't know you had.
CHESTER. Say, Zack, why don't you stay and play dominoes with us?
ZACHARY. I don't know how to play.
CHESTER. Come on. Any idiot can play. No offense meant. And there's dinner in it. This is our Thursday night ritual. We play dominoes and Mamma keeps a steady stream of food coming from the kitchen. When was the last time you had a square meal?
ZACHARY. If it's not an imposition.
CHESTER. If it's not an imposition! Zack, I think you're carrying this nice guy bit a little too far. Did you all hear that? Roxanne, get the box of dominoes. Let's clear the table. Pull up a chair. (*They seat themselves around the table.*) So Frankie, what's new? Anything exciting in the field of law-enforcement?
FRANKIE. Well, if you want news, there was a real mess over at the Prince Hotel.
CHESTER. Mess, what mess? I saw there was a crowd over there this afternoon.
FRANKIE. They found a woman's body cut up in four pieces.
CHESTER. Cut up in four pieces. Now how would you

do that? (*Draws imaginary lines on ROXANNE then, as she speaks, on himself*)

ROXANNE. Stop that!

MRS. NURDIGER. Horrible.

FRANKIE. They found the pieces in a trunk some guest had left behind.

ZACHARY. Have they caught the murderer?

FRANKIE. No, they don't have any idea who did it.

CHESTER. (*Laughs.*)

ZACHARY. And who was the victim?

FRANKIE. I'm afraid they don't know that either.

MRS. NURDIGER. You mean they can't even identify the victim?

FRANKIE. Her identity is a little hard to establish. You see, the body was naked and the head was missing.

CHESTER. Perhaps it was mislaid.

MRS. NURDIGER. Please, don't joke about it. It gives me chills just thinking about this woman cut up in four pieces.

CHESTER. We can laugh because we are here surrounded by friends, safe and sound. You have to admit some of these crimes are so grotesque they are almost funny.

MRS. NURDIGER. To you, perhaps.

CHESTER. What about the man in Chinatown who found a woman's toe in his chow mein.

ROXANNE. How did they know it was a woman's toe?

CHESTER. The toenail was painted—red!

MRS. NURDIGER. (*shudders*) Ehgh!

CHESTER. I read about a woman who bit into a piece of fried chicken and discovered it was a rat. She had a heart attack. But that's different I suppose. I mean it isn't murder.

ZACHARY. It's grisly none the less.

THE ARTIFICIAL JUNGLE 23

CHESTER. Where the devil do you think her head went? The woman who was quartered.

FRANKIE. We have no idea. It disappeared without a trace.

ZACHARY. Do many crimes go unpunished?

FRANKIE. Are you kidding? Stranglings, poisonings, drownings, and fatal falls—they disappear without a scream or so much as a drop of blood. And no weapon found. The police search. But they find no clues. And the murderer is walking around free as a bird.

PARROT. (*Screams, all jump with fright.*)

FRANKIE. Freer than some, I might add. These are in cages.

MRS. NURDIGER. But surely they always make some slip.

FRANKIE. No—the fact is some of them don't. There are murderers among us and we never know who they are. Why, I'm sure some of us meet a murderer every day. He could be your barber, the butcher or your dearest loved one.

MRS. NURDIGER. Oh nonsense! Enough of this talk. Are the police of no use at all, then?

FRANKIE. They're of use when they have clues. But when there are no clues—they can't do the impossible.

CHESTER. What do you think, Zack? Do you believe in the perfect crime? Do you think it's possible to commit a murder and get away with it?

ZACHARY. I think Frankie is trying to frighten us with his gruesome stories. If there are no clues and no bodies how can we be so sure these crimes were actually committed? I'm sure your wife is not so gullible. What do you think, Mrs. Nurdiger?

ROXANNE. What no one knows does not exist.

MRS. NURDIGER. Good heavens! Let's talk about

something else. What happened to your game of dominoes?

CHESTER. You're right, Mamma, we've forgotten to play. (*Dumps tiles. They shuffle and deal.*)

MRS. NURDIGER. I'll serve the cold cuts. (*Shivers.*) Oooh cold cuts. (*exits*)

CHESTER. Here we go. We each take seven. Who's high? Double Nine!—I'll be the first to go!

(*They play as the curtain falls.*)

ACT TWO

As before but the shop seems more lush. The piranha tank, in particular, has a new tropical look. CHESTER is dressed in a Tarzan costume and ZACHARY videotapes him. MRS. NURDIGER and ROXANNE look on admiringly.

ZACHARY. Ready, Chester?
CHESTER. Do you think this leopard skin is too sexy?
ROXANNE. Not at all.
CHESTER. It doesn't make me look fat?
ZACHARY. You look svelte.
CHESTER. I wish we could get the new sign in.
ZACHARY. You know the new sign won't be ready until later. Which reminds me you've got to pick it up this afternoon. Once it's up I'll get a shot of it to end the commercial. Okay now let's do it. Ready, Chester.
CHESTER. I'm nervous.
ZACHARY. Don't be. Just remember to get all the information in. And give it lots of personality.
CHESTER. Okay. Shoot.
ZACHARY. All right now. Lights. Camera. Action.
CHESTER. (*Lets out a Tarzan cry then speaks in an almost expressionless voice. He is no actor*) This is The Artificial Jungle. Bring love into your home with a cuddly pet or add a touch of the exotic with a home aquarium, tropical fish, a snake, lizard or even a tarantula. We have everything you need to bring adventure into your living room. Or take home a cuddly hamster, rat, mouse, or gerbil. Whatever your choice we have all the accessories to turn your home into an artificial jungle too.

Open six days a week. Conveniently located at 966 Rivington Street in lower Manhattan.

MRS. NURDIGER. (*having left during commercial, enters in a sarong*) I'm the Artificial Jungle mother. We have talking parrots too.

CHESTER. (*Lets out Tarzan cry again.*)

MRS. NURDIGER. My son the Orangutang.

ZACHARY. Cut! That's a good one.

CHESTER. Let's do it again. I mispronounced tarantula.

MRS. NURDIGER. Did you? I didn't notice.

CHESTER. I did. I said tarantyula.

ZACHARY. Nobody will notice.

CHESTER. You don't think?

ZACHARY. No. It was perfect.

CHESTER. If you say so. Did you hear that, Roxanne? Perfect! It was rather good.

ZACHARY. Now as soon as you pick up that sign I can get a shot of it for the end.

CHESTER. (*changing out of costume*) I'll go right away. I can't wait to see that sign in the window.

ZACHARY. I'll take the old one down and spruce up the shop a bit before you get back.

CHESTER. Fine. Roxanne, you take care of customers. Give Mamma a rest.

ROXANNE. Don't worry I've got everything under control.

CHESTER. (*exits whistling*) See you later.

MRS. NURDIGER. Chester left his Tarzan costume on the floor. (*Folding it.*) I'll put it away. He really was something in his Tarzan costume, wasn't he? (*exits*)

ROXANNE. I can't stand it anymore.

ZACHARY. Be patient, Roxy, it won't be long now.

ROXANNE. How can I be patient laying next to him at

THE ARTIFICIAL JUNGLE

night thinking about you. Wondering where you are, who you're with. Sometimes I think I'm going crazy.

ZACHARY. It isn't easy for me either, going home to a flop house laying on the bed counting the cracks in the ceiling and the roaches in the cracks. Trying to think of something else while all the time I can still smell you on me. You know I have a pair of your panties. I stole them. I always carry them with me. I caress them at night.

ROXANNE. Oh Zack, I'd do anything for you.

ZACHARY. Would you blow?

ROXANNE. Sure.

ZACHARY. I mean leave here, run away with me tonight.

ROXANNE. No, I couldn't.

MRS. NURDIGER. (*Enters to fuss with various shop items.*)

ROXANNE. And the ram horn snails are fifty cents apiece . . .

MRS. NURDIGER. (*Exits*)

ZACHARY. We could hit the road — live like a couple of bums.

ROXANNE. That's okay for kids. But we're at the age when we like our creature comforts. I can't run away and become a gypsy. Not now. How I hate him.

ZACHARY. Why did you marry him?

ROXANNE. He's the only one who asked.

ZACHARY. You've gotta be kidding! A dame with your looks?

ROXANNE. Oh there were others. But they just didn't stand on ceremony. I got invited to a lot of parties. And I used to go. A lot of parties for two.

ZACHARY. I figured you'd been around the block.

ROXANNE. I didn't get these lips from suckin' doorknobs.

MRS. NURDIGER. (*Enters as before.*)

ROXANNE. Here are the aquatic plants: the anacrus and the cabamba, the hydrophyla and the water sprite. They are priced as marked. You put them in a plastic bag and tie them off like this. (*Demonstrates.*) Now here are the feeder goldfish.

MRS. NURDIGER. (*Exits*)

ZACHARY. You like me, don't you?

ROXANNE. Oh yes. I like you. I like you fine. You smell like a man. He smells like a bar of soap. Watch it!

MRS. NURDIGER. (*enters*) I think the rats are in heat. Are either of you hungry? I could make lunch.

ROXANNE. No, wait for Chester.

MRS. NURDIGER. Then I'll just go to your room and watch my program. (*exits*)

ROXANNE. Let's do it.

ZACHARY. What?

ROXANNE. What we talked about.

ZACHARY. You can fry for that.

ROXANNE. Not in New York State. There's a law against capital punishment.

ZACHARY. So you get life.

ROXANNE. Not if you do it right. You heard what Frankie said.

ZACHARY. But I've got nothing against this guy.

ROXANNE. No? Even though he's standing in our way? While you spend your lonely nights counting cracks, he's banging the woman you love.

ZACHARY. Now that you put it that way.

ROXANNE. We've all got to go someday. Death can be awaited or it can be induced. What's the difference when it comes when come it must?

ZACHARY. You talk as though it were perfectly alright.

ROXANNE. No one will know but you and me. We'll

be the judges. We'll be the jury. No one will know but us. And what no one knows does not exist. Now kiss me, Zack. Kiss me till I bleed.

ZACHARY. You're like a wild animal.

ROXANNE. In an artificial jungle. (*They kiss.*)

(*CHESTER'S whistling is heard.*)

CHESTER. Just wait until you get a load of this sign. Here help me unpack it. Gently gently. The thing cost an arm and a leg. It breaks if you look at it crosswise. (*Unpacks sign and displays it proudly.*)

ZACHARY. You didn't tell me about the palm trees.

ROXANNE. Or the parrots.

CHESTER. They were my idea. Mamma! Mamma! Look at this.

MRS. NURDIGER. (*enters*) Why Chester it's lovely. Real artistic.

CHESTER. I can't wait to hang it in that window. I'm going to get a ladder.

MRS. NURDIGER. Have you eaten?

CHESTER. No.

MRS. NURDIGER. (*as they exit*) I saved you plenty.

ROXANNE. Do you have that insurance policy here?

ZACHARY. Yes. But how are we going to get him to sign?

ROXANNE. Leave that to me.

CHESTER. Here we go. (*Brings in ladder.*)

ROXANNE. Oh, Chester, the Reptile Supplier was here, he wants you to sign this invoice.

CHESTER. Let me see that. I never sign anything without reading it first. (*Reads.*) Iguanas—two, horned lizards six, one was dead.

ROXANNE. He gave you credit.

CHESTER. Oh yes. Three skinks, baby boa, corn snake, indigo, turtles red eared sliders, box. Everything seems to be in order. (*Signs.*) Here you go. (*Sets up ladder and starts to climb.*)

ROXANNE. He wants you to sign two copies.

CHESTER. Isn't there a carbon there?

ROXANNE. Yes but he wants an extra one for his file.

CHESTER. Duplicate, triplicate, the paper work expands but does anything more get accomplished? Where is it? (*Descends the ladder.*)

ROXANNE. Here. (*She slides the top copy up just enough to leave room for him to sign. He signs and ROXANNE and ZACHARY exchange a look*)

CHESTER. (*climbing the ladder again and taking down the old sign*) Out with the old and in with the new. (*Hangs the new sign in the window and almost falls — ZACK catches the ladder just in time.*) Zack, hold the ladder you wouldn't want me to fall and kill myself, would you?

ZACHARY. Of course not. (*Aside*) Now what did I go and do that for?

CHESTER. Here, Roxanne, plug it in. And be careful of those wires around the aquariums. Somebody could get electrocuted.

ROXANNE. (*dipping the plug in water*) Here you do it. I'm afraid.

CHESTER. Alright. (*Plugs in sign, all the lights go out.*) We must have blown a fuse. I'll have to go down to the basement. (*exits with flashlight*)

ROXANNE. This is our chance. It's dark. Follow him downstairs and hit him over the head. It will look like he fell.

ZACHARY. What will I hit him with?

ROXANNE. (*takes a decorative rock off the shelf*) Here's a rock.

THE ARTIFICIAL JUNGLE

ZACHARY. (*takes rock and follows CHESTER out*) Let me help. Chester, be careful on those stairs in the dark!

(*loud blow is heard off*)

CHESTER. Ow!
ZACHARY. What happened?
MRS. NURDIGER. (*entering*) What's the matter? (*The lights come on.*)
CHESTER. (*Reentering with ZACK*) I seem to have hit my head on something. (*Shows lump.*)
MRS. NURDIGER. You've got an egg on your head. Kiss and make better.
ROXANNE. (*aside to ZACHARY*) You didn't hit him hard enough.
ZACHARY. I hit him with all my might.
ROXANNE. If we're going to do this we've got to do it right. No more slip-ups.
ZACHARY. He must have a head like a sledgehammer. Look at this rock. (*Shows rock broken in two pieces.*)
MRS. NURDIGER. What did I tell you? There's going to be a lump. You lie down and I'll put some ice on it. (*She goes to kitchen. CHESTER lies down on bed.*)
ROXANNE. Did he see you do it?
ZACHARY. No, I don't think so. The lights were out. I hit him from behind.
ROXANNE. I'm telling you there can't be any more slip-ups.
ZACHARY. If you hate this guy so much why stick around? We could split. Hit the road. Live like a couple of gypsies.
ROXANNE. Are you crazy? We've got him insured for a hundred grand. All we've got to do is cash him in.
ZACHARY. Never again.

ROXANNE. Listen, Zack, he's accident prone. We have to plan it better that's all. Throw 'em off our trail. Put the blame somewhere else.

ZACHARY. Like where?

ROXANNE. Like on the piranhas. They can strip a body in half an hour and they do a clean job. Nobody ever sent a piranha up the river.

ZACHARY. You're sick, Lady.

ROXANNE. Love is the disease. And you gave it to me.

ZACHARY. Look, Roxy, you can't get away with it.

ROXANNE. We can if we do it right. Tonight after closing time I'll slip him a mickey. There's lots of stuff in the shop that he could take by accident. Run this insurance policy down to the corner and drop it in the mailbox. The last pick up is at six. It will be postmarked today. After midnight we'll cash him in.

ZACHARY. What do you think I am?

ROXANNE. Kiss me and I'll tell you. (*They kiss.*) Kiss me harder. (*They kiss again.*) Bite me. Make me bleed. (*They kiss until blood spurts.*) You still wanna know what I think you are?

ZACHARY. Yeah?

ROXANNE. A killer. (*Licks a stamp and puts it on the letter.*) Now mail this and come back right away. Tonight we're going to do it. And we're going to do it right.

MRS. NURDIGER. (*at CHESTER'S bedside*) What happened to you?

CHESTER. (*groans*) Ow my head!

MRS. NURDIGER. Son, tell me, what did you do?

CHESTER. I must have hit my head on a pipe. It was dark. Then it was darker. Except for the little stars.

ZACHARY. (*who has been overhearing this conversation with ROXANNE*) Do you think she's suspicious?

ROXANNE. No, she's a trusting old soul. It's almost

THE ARTIFICIAL JUNGLE 33

closing time. Go and come back quickly, before I have to close up.

(*ZACHARY starts out the shop door with the stamped envelope containing the signed insurance policy. MRS. NURDIGER enters. ZACHARY hides the envelope behind his back.*)

MRS. NURDIGER. Go get into your nightie, Chester. Where are you going, Mr. Slade?
ZACHARY. I er was just going out to ah . . .
ROXANNE. Get some wine. I thought we ought to celebrate.
MRS. NURDIGER. Celebrate?
ROXANNE. Yes, the new piranha tank, the neon sign, The Artificial Jungle. It seems we have a lot to celebrate, don't we?
MRS. NURDIGER. (*dubiously*) Yes, I suppose we do.
ROXANNE. And Mr. Slade, hurry back with that wine. And make sure it's the very best. My husband deserves nothing but the best. Here's some cash. There's a liquor store around the corner. Go. (*With hidden significance.*) It's almost six o'clock.
MRS. NURDIGER. I'm worried about Chester. He may have a fractured skull.
ROXANNE. Don't worry yourself unnecessarily, Mother Nurdiger. He got a bump on the head, that's all.
MRS. NURDIGER. Perhaps Mr. Slade could go for a doctor. Or we could take him to Beth Israel.
ROXANNE. I'm sure he'll be alright after he's had a good night's sleep.
MRS. NURDIGER. But that's just it. I've heard that sometimes, if they fall asleep with a fractured skull— they don't wake up.

ROXANNE. (*exchanges a significant look with ZA-CHARY, then looks at her watch*) It's quarter to six. The liquor store is going to close. Hurry, *Mr. Slade* and get that wine.

(*ZACHARY stands frozen for a moment and then realizing she means the mail pick-up dashes out the door*)

MRS. NURDIGER. You don't think we should take him to the hospital?

ROXANNE. If he doesn't feel better by tomorrow, yes. But tomorrow his pain may be over and he'll be as good as new.

MRS. NURDIGER. I hope so. Did you see the size of that lump on his head? Poor Chester, he's always been accident prone.

ROXANNE. Yes, accident prone. You've always said that yourself, haven't you?

MRS. NURDIGER. Well, you know: He was dropped by his nurse, he was hit by a car, he was thrown by a horse, he fell off his bike and got a scar under his chin. He got a fishhook caught in his finger, he broke his arm, he broke his leg, he got a tooth knocked out in a fight, sprained his ankle, he sprained his neck, he almost drowned, he slipped on ice . . . he burned himself on an iron, he fell down the stairs, he's been bitten or stung by every kind of animal you can imagine and now, I'm afraid he's fractured his skull. God, when you come to think of it, he's probably the luckiest man alive.

ROXANNE. Lucky?

MRS. NURDIGER. To have survived all those accidents. Why any one of them would have been enough to kill him.

CHESTER. (*groans*) Ow, my head!

THE ARTIFICIAL JUNGLE

Mrs. Nurdiger. I'd better go look in on him (*goes to CHESTER*)

(*ZACHARY enters with bottle of wine.*)

Roxanne. Did you mail it?
Zachary. Yes, and as I was coming back I saw the mailman pick it up.
Roxanne. Good, then we're in business.
Zachary. Here's the wine. The best they had.
Roxanne. Chateau Lafitte 1972. I hope that was a better year for wine than it was for me. That was the year I married him.
Zachary. Look, I'm getting cold feet. Let's stop this before it goes any further.
Roxanne. Don't you want me?
Zachary. You know I do.
Roxanne. Don't you want us to be together?
Zachary. I'm aching for it.
Roxanne. Me too. Don't you see? This is the only way.
Zachary. Is that the only way? To kill a man for his pet shop and his wife?
Roxanne. Wash your mouth out with soap. Wife is a dirty four-letter word. I'm his whore! I'm his maid!
Zachary. I don't care! That's your business. Yours and his. Leave me out of it!
Roxanne. You don't care? Even when he comes home with the stink of liquor on his breath and beats me.
Zachary. He beats you? Chester? But he wouldn't hurt a fly.
Roxanne. Not unless he happened to bore it to death.
Zachary. What if I go to jail?
Roxanne. I'd wait for you. Wouldn't you wait for me?

ZACHARY. Yes, yes, yes.
ROXANNE. Now let's kiss and kill. (*They kiss.*)
PARROT. Gawk! Where's Roxanne? Where's Roxanne? Gawk! I spy! I spy!
ZACHARY. What was that? A parrot?
ROXANNE. That's just Chester playing. He's an amateur ventriloquist. That's how he sells birds that don't talk to suckers. He throws his voice into the bird and they buy. Of course we have a no refund policy.
ZACHARY. The birds don't talk, huh?
ROXANNE. No they're all too old to learn. In the shop they talk but when the people get them home they clam up.
ZACHARY. The little crook.
ROXANNE. Yeah, he's a little crook and a cheapskate too. I'm lucky if I get a new dress twice a year.
ZACHARY. Still you look hot.
ROXANNE. After we cash him in I'll look hotter. And it will be all yours baby. All yours. (*They go to the living area behind shop.*)
MRS. NURDIGER. (*carrying a tray*) Chester is going to take his supper in bed.
ROXANNE. Yes, let us help you spoil him. Mr. Slade, bring that wine. I'll get some glasses.
MRS. NURDIGER. I'll get them.
ROXANNE. No, no, you let me do it. You're always waiting on us hand and foot. You go to Chester.
MRS. NURDIGER. Why, Roxanne, what's come over you? (*She goes to CHESTER*) Chester, we're going to have a little drink to celebrate the new sign. Here, put this ice pack on your head.
ROXANNE. This ought to do it.
ZACHARY. What's that?
ROXANNE. Malachite Green. Its a cure for ich.
ZACHARY. Ich?

THE ARTIFICIAL JUNGLE

ROXANNE. Yeah it's a disease in tropical fish. They get a white fuzz all over them. (*Reads label.*) Malachite Green controls ich in tropical fish. CAUTION: Keep out of the reach of children. Also poisonous to baby fish and Tetra Species. Pour the wine. (*Zachary does so.*) Now we have to make sure he gets this glass. (*She pours a dollop of Malachite Green into the glass intended for Chester.*)

CHESTER. The new neon sign does look beautiful, doesn't it, Mamma?

MRS. NURDIGER. It looks real gorgeous.

CHESTER. And the custom-made decor piranha tank sure is swell too, isn't it?

MRS. NURDIGER. It's the prettiest piranha tank I've ever seen.

CHESTER. Me either. Oh, Mamma, I never thought such happiness could exist in this world.

MRS. NURDIGER. God has been good to us.

CHESTER. You know it's all Zack's doing. He's such a nice guy. He's really come to be like one of the family. Don't you feel that way too, Mamma?

MRS. NURDIGER. Yes, Chester, I do. Now you rest. Don't exert yourself unnecessarily because that may be a concussion.

CHESTER. Don't worry about it. You know I'm accident prone. Did you see when that ladder started to go over? It's a good thing Zack was there to break my fall.

(*ROXANNE and ZACHARY enter with the tray of glasses into which the wine has been poured.*)

ROXANNE. (*passing the glasses around*) May I propose a toast?

CHESTER. Yes, a toast! Roxanne, a toast! (*Winces.*) Oooh, my head.

MRS. NURDIGER. Easy, Chester.

ROXANNE. To the new neon sign, to the Artificial Jungle, and to the piranhas! (*All raise glasses.*)

MRS. NURDIGER. To the piranhas? Why toast the piranhas?

CHESTER. Why not toast the piranhas, Mamma! That's a very good toast. To the piranhas, the king of the tetras.

ROXANNE. Tetras? Piranhas aren't tetras.

CHESTER. Oh yes they are! They are the greater tetras. And I drink to them! (*Goes to drink.*)

ZACHARY. (*stopping CHESTER from drinking*) Chester, there's some cork in your wine. Let me get you another glass. (*Takes CHESTER's glass and goes to the kitchen and pours him another.*)

CHESTER. Cork? I didn't notice any. Zack is so thoughtful.

MRS. NURDIGER. He's a real gentleman.

ROXANNE. All he does is eat our food.

CHESTER. I don't know what you have against him, Roxanne. I wish you liked him better.

ZACHARY. Here's a fresh glass, Chester.

CHESTER. Thank you, Zack. That was very considerate. Now I forgot the toast. (*Raises his glass*) To our pet shop, The Artificial Jungle, wasn't that it, Roxanne?

ROXANNE. Yes, to our pet shop!

CHESTER. Say, that was good!

ZACHARY. You want to see the label?

CHESTER. All wines are the same. They just put the fancy label on to get your money. Chateau Lafitte 1972. It's an omen! That was the year we were married!

MRS. NURDIGER. How's your head doing, sweetie?

CHESTER. Well it's still pretty sore. But it feels better since I've had this wine.

ROXANNE. Have another glass.

THE ARTIFICIAL JUNGLE

CHESTER. Don't mind if I do.

MRS. NURDIGER. Chester, honey, go easy on the wine. It may not be good after a bump on the head.

ROXANNE. It can't be bad if it lessens the pain. (*refills CHESTER's glass*)

MRS. NURDIGER. Alright one more but after that put it away. You know you have a tendency to overdo.

CHESTER. Alright, Mamma, just one more for medicinal porpoises. (*Drinks.*)

MRS. NURDIGER. Now why don't we all leave Chester alone to rest so that he'll be bright-eyed and bushy-tailed tomorrow. (*They leave the bedroom.*)

ZACHARY. I'll be going.

ROXANNE. I'll let you out and lock up.

MRS. NURDICER. I could use a good night's sleep myself. I just hope the garbage trucks don't wake me up at the crack of dawn.

ROXANNE. They won't if you turn off your hearing aid.

MRS. NURDIGER. That's a good idea. But then I won't be able to hear Chester if he calls out during the night.

ROXANNE. Don't worry I'll be here to take care of him. I promise I'll wake you if there's any need.

MRS. NURDIGER. Alright I'll turn my hearing aid off. I do tend to be a light sleeper. (*Turns off hearing aid.*)

ZACHARY. Good night, Mrs. Nurdiger.

MRS. NURDIGER. (*shouting*) How's that?

ZACHARY. (*shouting likewise*) I said good night, Mrs. Nurdiger.

MRS. NURDIGER. What did you say? Oh my, I can't hear a thing without my hearing aid. (*Turns it back on.*) There, now what did you say?

ZACHARY. I said, good night, Mrs. Nurdiger.

MRS. NURDIGER. Good night, Mr. Slade. Zack. I'm

calling you Zack, if it's all right with you. Because Chester says you're like one of the family. Do you like it?

ZACHARY. Yes, I like it, Mrs. Nurdiger. I like it fine.

MRS. NURDIGER. And I wish that from now on you'd call me Mother Nurdiger. Would you do that? For me?

ZACHARY. Yes, thank you, Mother Nurdiger.

MRS. NURDIGER. Now don't talk to me, I'm turning this thing off and going to bed. (*Turns off hearing aid and exits*)

ROXANNE. That's great. You've got the old lady eating out of the palm of your hand.

ZACHARY. That was a close one with the wine.

ROXANNE. Yeah we almost poisoned some perfectly good piranhas but what's worse is we almost poisoned our alibi. I didn't know piranhas were tetras.

ZACHARY. You learn something every day. Now what are we going to do? We can't poison him.

ROXANNE. No we'll have to smother him in his sleep. You go and come back in about half an hour. Tap on my window. By then I'll have him good and drunk, you'll be able to overpower him. I'll give you a signal. I'll whistle softly.

ZACHARY. What if he cries out and somebody comes to help him?

ROXANNE. Are you kidding? This is New York City. Go. (*Loudly*) Good night. And don't be late tomorrow. We've got a big fish delivery.

ZACHARY. Okay. Good night. Good night, Chester. (*exits*)

CHESTER. Good night, Zack.

(*ROXANNE goes back to the bedroom. CHESTER has been drinking all the wine and is now quite drunk and incoherent.*)

THE ARTIFICIAL JUNGLE 41

ROXANNE. (*softly*) Chester? Chester are you awake?

CHESTER. Yeah, c'mere, Roxanne. Gimme a big wet kiss.

ROXANNE. I don't want to.

CHESTER. Come on. (*Tries to grab her.*)

ROXANNE. Not tonight, Chester. I have a headache.

CHESTER. So take an aspirin.

ROXANNE. Please, Chester, I'm not in the mood.

CHESTER. (*drunkenly*) Let's have another glash of wine. A post to the tiranahs. Zzzzzzzzzz. (*He is asleep.*)

ROXANNE. (*softly*) Chester? (*Shakes him gently.*) Chester? (*She pauses a moment to listen and then she whistles softly. There is no response. She lays there staring at the ceiling. We hear only the sound of CHESTER snoring. After a pause she whistles again softly. There is a light tapping at the window. She gets up and opens the window. ZACK climbs in.*)

ZACHARY. Now what?

ROXANNE. Like we planned.

ZACHARY. Are you sure you want to go through with it?

ROXANNE. Sure I'm sure. Are you sure?

ZACHARY. I'm sure if you're sure.

ROXANNE. Then do it. Here's a pillow.

ZACHARY. (*takes pillow and raises it over CHESTER's sleeping face*) Here goes. (*Pauses.*) I can't do it.

ROXANNE. You've got to do it. We've come this far. We can't turn back now.

ZACHARY. I can't.

ROXANNE. Listen, Zack, we're on this train together and we're not getting off until the last stop.

CHESTER. (*suddenly waking and not fully realizing where he is sees ZACK standing over him*) Hi, Zack, want shome more wine—Hey, Roxanne, get another glass. A toast to — Hey, wait a minute — What time is it? I must have . . . What are you doing here? What are you doing? (*ZACHARY smothers CHESTER with the pillow*) Hey, Zack, cut it out! Ha! Ha! Stop it. That isn't funny. I can't breathe. I CAN'T BREATHE! Stop! Help! Zack! Roxanne, help me! Roxanne! (*He manages to get out from under the pillow and sees that Roxanne is staring at him coldly.*) Roxanne. Roxanne. (*ZACHARY holds the pillow over CHESTER's face again.*) Mamma! Mamma! Roxanne! (*He coughs and we hear his muffled cries through the pillow. Finally the sounds fade and he stops. ROXANNE and ZACHARY exchange a look. She nods. ZACHARY removes the pillow from CHESTER's face. CHESTER jumps up and starts screaming again*) Help! Help! Aahhhgh! (*ZACHARY smothers him again. This time he dies.*)

ROXANNE. Now let's get him into that piranha tank.
ZACHARY. I hope those piranhas are hungry.
ROXANNE. They should be. I haven't fed them in a week.

(*With difficulty they lift CHESTER'S body and lug it to the piranha tank. They lift him over it and, just as they are about to dump him in, a flashlight is seen through the pet shop window. Footsteps are heard. FRANKIE, the cop on the beat, in his uniform is outside. ROXANNE and ZACHARY quickly drop CHESTER on the floor. FRANKIE taps on the door. ZACHARY jumps back behind the shop door just as ROXANNE opens it.*)

FRANKIE. I heard some sounds and saw you were awake. Did you know your bedroom window is open?
ROXANNE. I was just trying to get some air.

THE ARTIFICIAL JUNGLE   43

FRANKIE. (*seeing CHESTER on the floor*) What happened to Chester?

ROXANNE. He polished off a whole bottle of wine.

FRANKIE. That's Chester. Never knows his limit. Let me help you get him into bed.

ROXANNE. I hate to put you to all this trouble.

FRANKIE. Oh it's no trouble. It's all in the line of duty. Besides Chester is a pal. Come on, you take his legs. Alley Ooop! God, he sure is loaded isn't he? It's like trying to lift a dead weight.

ROXANNE. Yeah, you can say that again. (*They lug him to the bed and tuck him in.*)

FRANKIE. I guess there's nothing he can do but sleep it off. Good night, Chester.

(*ROXANNE waves CHESTER's hand at FRANKIE. All this time ZACHARY has been hiding behind the open shop door.*)

FRANKIE. (*as he starts to leave shines his flashlight all over the door and then lets it come to rest on the lock and handle*) You should consider getting a better lock for this door — a police lock — there have been a lot of burglaries in the neighborhood lately. (*As he speaks he opens and closes the door revealing and concealing ZACHARY whom he just misses seeing.*) Talk to Chester about it.

ROXANNE. Yeah, I'll talk to Chester about it.

FRANKIE. Good night, Roxanne.

ROXANNE. Good night, Frankie. (*She closes the door after him.*)

(*ZACHARY is plastered against the wall behind the door, frozen in terror. Just as he starts to move, FRANKIE reopens the door and pokes his head in.*)

FRANKIE. Tell Chester — raw egg and tomato juice and a dash of tabasco sauce — good cure for a hangover.
ROXANNE. Yes.
FRANKIE. (*closes door to leave then opens it again*) Or if all else fails — hair of the dog that bit him.
ROXANNE. Yeah, yeah. Hair of the dog.

(*FRANKIE leaves and walks off. The sound of his whistling gradually fades in the distance.*)

ROXANNE. It's clear. He's gone.
ZACHARY. What if he comes back?
ROXANNE. He won't. Now we've got to get him into that tank.

(*They carry CHESTER to the piranha tank and dump him in. Sounds of the piranhas eating as the lights fade.*)

ACT THREE

Several days later. ROXANNE is working around the shop. ZACHARY enters with a box.

ROXANNE. Zack, the insurance money came through.
ZACHARY. Look, I bought you this. (*slips a fur jacket over her shoulders*)
ROXANNE. Oh, Zack, is it mink?
ZACHARY. No, skunk.
ROXANNE. We're rich now, Zack. Everything has worked out just the way we planned.
ZACHARY. I just can't get over the way he looked when they fished him out of the piranha tank! I thought you said they did a clean job.
ROXANNE. They do. But Chester was only partially submerged. We had to make it look like an accident.
ZACHARY. His face was hideously eaten away. How's Mother Nurdiger?
ROXANNE. Oh, she's alright. She has her good days and her bad days.
ZACHARY. She really took it hard.
ROXANNE. Chester was her baby. Every time she thinks of him or hears his name she starts that crying. Try not to mention him if you can avoid it.

MRS. NURDIGER. (*enters*) Oh, Zack, you're here. Thank you so much for all your help in our troubled time. I just don't think I could have handled the funeral arrangements myself.
ZACHARY. Why should you have to?
MRS. NURDIGER. Oh, you're so kind. I don't know

how to thank you. Not only for myself—but for Chester . . . Chester thanks you too. (*She weeps.*)

ROXANNE. (*showing impatience*) What did I tell you?

ZACHARY. There there.

MRS. NURDIGER. I don't know what I would have done without you. Chester was right. You're like one of the family. (*Weeps.*) Where are you going, Roxanne?

ROXANNE. I was just going to feed the piranhas.

MRS. NURDIGER. (*recoils with horror*) The piranhas? Why should you feed them? I hate them! I hate them! They killed my baby! They killed my baby! (*She attacks the piranha tank, bursts into tears, and sinks to the floor, feebly beating on the tank with her fists and weeping.*)

ROXANNE. Now, now, Mother Nurdiger, it wasn't their fault. They didn't know what they were doing.

MRS. NURDIGER. They're evil! Evil murderers! Evil murderers!

ZACHARY. They're just dumb animals. They kill by instinct. They have no moral sense.

ROXANNE. And no remorse.

MRS. NURDIGER. I could kill them with my bare hands. (*Goes to put her hands in the tank.*)

ZACHARY. (*stopping her in the nick of time*) I wouldn't do that if I were you.

MRS. NURDIGER. Why should they live when they killed my Chester. Chester! Oh. (*Weeps.*)

ROXANNE. Oh, here comes Mrs. Muncie to buy the weekly rat for her boa constrictor. Come now, Mother Nurdiger, you don't want Mrs. Muncie to see you like this. Zack, help her to her room.

MRS. NURDIGER. Oh, you're so kind. I know that Chester is up in heaven looking down on your kindness. I know he's seen everything you've done. I know he

THE ARTIFICIAL JUNGLE

blesses you both and he'll ask God to repay you for it. (*ZACHARY helps her off*)

(*MRS. MUNCIE enters the shop as in Act I. Because her shawl is over her head we do not see her face.*)

ROXANNE. (*waits on her*) The usual, Mrs. Muncie?

(*MRS. MUNCIE nods*)

ROXANNE. We've got a beautiful rat for you today — nice and fat. (*She gets rat. ZACHARY reenters*)
ROXANNE. How is she?
ZACHARY. She's resting. Oh hello, and how are you today, Mrs. Muncie?
MRS. MUNCIE. (*turns, it is CHESTER with part of his face eaten away*) As well as can be expected, Mr. Slade. And how are you?
ZACHARY. (*frozen in horror*) Oh God! Oh God! It can't be!
ROXANNE. What is it?
ZACHARY. Look there! Look there! (*Points to MRS. MUNCIE.*) Don't you see who it is?
ROXANNE. Yes, Zack, it's Mrs. Muncie.
ZACHARY. No! No! It's him! It's him! Chester! Chester!
MRS. MUNCIE. (*to ROXANNE*) The young man seems to have mistaken me for someone else.
ROXANNE. Here, Mrs. Muncie, take the rat — there'll be no charge today. (*Hurries her out of the shop.*) Good day, Mrs. Muncie, good day! (*Slams the shop door and locks it.*) What's gotten into you? You frightened that poor old lady half to death.

ZACHARY. Old lady? Old lady? (*Laughs insanely.*) That was no old lady. It was Chester. Didn't you see how his face was eaten away by the piranhas?

ROXANNE. Zack, you've got to get hold of yourself. You're seeing things.

ZACHARY. No. No. I'm not seeing things! It was Chester, I tell you! It was Chester!

ROXANNE. (*in a hoarse whisper*) Quiet! Do you want to give us away? I'm going to close the shop. It's been a long day and we're all under a strain.

ZACHARY. I tell you it was Chester.

ROXANNE. Stop saying that. It was Mrs. Muncie. I hope she doesn't talk about it. It might arouse suspicions.

ZACHARY. I'm sorry — I must be losing my grip. I could have sworn I saw —

ROXANNE. (*interrupting him*) Now that's enough about what you thought you saw. Go into my room and lie down for a while. I'll get you a good stiff drink.

ZACHARY. Yes, yes, that's what I need — a good stiff drink. (*He goes and lays on the bed, turns on the t.v., and hears the first few lines from CHESTER's Act II commercial before snapping it off. Roxanne pours a shot of whiskey, tosses it down, then brings him the bottle and shot glass. He quickly throws down three shots.*)

ROXANNE. Feel steadier?

ZACHARY. Yeah. Give me another.

ROXANNE. That's enough. We can't take the risk of getting loaded and talking too much now can we?

ZACHARY. No, no — What have you made me do? What have you made me do?

ROXANNE. What have *I* made you do?

ZACHARY. Yes, I killed the only person who ever gave me a break. I had nothing against him. It's all your fault.

ROXANNE. My fault? I like that! Did I force you to

climb in the window? Did I put the pillow in your hand? Did I force you to hold that pillow over his face while he gasped and begged for air? Did I make you choke the life out of him?

ZACHARY. (*covering his ears*) Stop! Stop! I don't want to hear any more!

ROXANNE. Well you'd better hear and you'd better hear good. You're the one who did it. Do you hear me? You're the one. I helped you plan it. But that was all.

ZACHARY. Don't say that. Don't put it that way. I thought we were on this train together—right until the very last stop.

ROXANNE. Yeah, we're on it together; and we'd better stay on it just as long as we can. Because the last stop is the cemetery.

ZACHARY. I've got to have another drink.

ROXANNE. (*taking the bottle away from him*) I said no more.

ZACHARY. I saw him. I saw him clear as day. And did you hear what he said to me? He asked me how I was!

ROXANNE. I tell you that was Mrs. Muncie. Come on now, Zack. Let's forget all that now. We've got each other, Zack, and that's all that matters. We've got each other—just the two of us—and nothing can ever come between us. (*Laying back on the bed behind him.*) Make love to me, Zack, and let me make you forget everything that ever was for good. (*She reaches to draw him to her. He turns to kiss her but it is CHESTER*)

ZACHARY. (*screams*) Chester! It's Chester! (*He tries to strangle CHESTER who disappears. He is strangling ROXANNE.*) Leave me alone, Chester! Leave me alone! I'll kill you again! I'll kill you a thousand times and a thousand different ways!

ROXANNE. Zack, please, I can't breathe. Zack! Zack,

please, My God! I don't dare call for help!

MRS. NURDIGER. (*rushes in and sees ZACHARY strangling ROXANNE*) What is it? What happened?

ZACHARY. (*raving at ROXANNE as he strangles her*) You're dead, Chester! Now you've got to lie down! Down in that grave we buried you in! Because you're dead, Chester! We killed you. We smothered you with your pillow and fed you to the piranhas! So lie down, Chester! You've got to lie down!

MRS. NURDIGER. You killed him? You killed my Chester. Murderers! Murderers! (*She staggers toward them.*) You killed my child. My poor little boy! Murderers! You murderers! Oh God, punish them! Punish them! (*Suddenly she is stricken and goes all crooked. She falls. ZACHARY releases ROXANNE and runs to her.*) I can't . . . I can't . . .

ZACHARY. Mother Nurdiger?

ROXANNE. She's dead.

ZACHARY. No. She's had a stroke. She's paralyzed. Her eyes are alive and they are threatening us.

ROXANNE. May God turn her lips and tongue to stone.

Blackout

ACT FOUR

It is a Thursday night—domino night several months later.

ROXANNE. Where are you going?
ZACHARY. To get Mother Nurdiger.
ROXANNE. Can't you leave her in her room?
ZACHARY. Have you forgotten? It's domino night.
ROXANNE. Domino night! How long must we go on with that infernal ritual?
ZACHARY. I know it's a strain. But we agreed that it was best to maintain the appearance of normalcy.
ROXANNE. Normalcy! Normalcy! We killed him to escape the tedium of existence. Now we're even more mired in it.
ZACHARY. It's only Frankie—faithful Frankie. And we do owe him something don't you think?
ROXANNE. (*with bitter irony*) Yes, I suppose we do.
ZACHARY. Because if he hadn't happened in on us it might have looked like murder. He was your witness that Chester was drunk and probably fell into the piranha tank and got himself killed. He was your air-tight alibi.
ROXANNE. Air-tight, yes.
ZACHARY. And it didn't hurt that he was an officer of the law.
ROXANNE. Yes, the law was on our side.
ZACHARY. And it's touching, his devotion to Mother Nurdiger.
ROXANNE. Yes, I know it's her he comes to see.
ZACHARY. So I'd better bring her out.
ROXANNE. I can't stand her eyes. They seem to be accusing us—damning us. She hates us. I know she'd tell everything if she could.

ZACHARY. Well, she can't. The paralysis is almost total. She can't move at all — except for her eyes.

ROXANNE. Her eyes! Her eyes! She's learned to make them speak and I know she accuses and damns us.

ZACHARY. It's almost time. Frankie will be here. I must get her.

ROXANNE. If you must — you must!

(*ZACHARY goes to get MOTHER NURDIGER whom he carries in and places in her usual chair at the table. She doesn't move a muscle — except for her eyes*)

ZACHARY. Here she comes! There you go, right in your usual chair, Mother Nurdiger. Are you comfortable? I think she says yes.

ROXANNE. I suppose she imagines us abandoning ourselves to our lust — our lust! — some joke!

ZACHARY. Do you have to rub it in?

ROXANNE. We killed him so we could be together — But there hasn't been anything between us since he's been out of the way. You haven't touched me since he died.

ZACHARY. I can't. I can't. He's there. Always there.

ROXANNE. That first night I went out and walked the streets. I made it with the first man I met. And I've done it since and been paid for it. In doorways, in cars, and in hotel rooms. I tried to forget. But always I thought of the woman who was cut up in four pieces. I was afraid. But sometimes I wished for it. Are you listening? Did you hear what I said to you? Any man would be furious. Aren't you furious? Why don't you beat me? Or aren't you a man at all?

ZACHARY. I'm relieved. It takes the pressure off of

THE ARTIFICIAL JUNGLE

me . . . the pressure to perform. (*He pauses then in alarm.*) My God. We've dropped our guard completely. We've been talking freely in front of her.

ROXANNE. She's so silent, like a statue. It's so easy to forget she's there.

ZACHARY. Look, look at her eyes. Her eyes are full of hatred.

ROXANNE. (*slightly mad*) No, no, not hatred. Sometimes I see great compassion in them. Her eyes speak to me. I understand the meaning of her every glance. I know she understands and has found it in her heart to forgive us. Isn't that right, Mother Nurdiger? You do forgive us, don't you? Look, her eyes are brimming over. She does forgive us. I know she does.

ZACHARY. No, you're deluding yourself. That's not a blessing you see in her eyes. It's a mother's curse. She is clinging to life in the hopes of seeing us punished. That's what keeps her going. Her hatred is keeping her alive and her desire for revenge.

ROXANNE. By God, I'll put those eyes out! (*She grabs an icepick.*)

ZACHARY. No! Do you want to give us away? (*struggles with her*) Drop that icepick! Drop it! (*ROXANNE drops the icepick*)

ROXANNE. So, you're afraid of being found out, you coward! I have a good mind to go to the police and tell them everything. It would be a relief. Yes, that's what I'll do. I'll go to the police right now. I'll tell them everything.

ZACHARY. You little fool! Are you crazy? You're not going anywhere.

ROXANNE. (*raving*) Coward! Coward! Coward! Coward!

ZACHARY. Look, she's listening. She knows everything that goes on in this house. I can't stand it anymore. I'm going to tell the police myself!

ROXANNE. Go, see if I care!

ZACHARY. (*putting on his jacket*) I will!

ROXANNE. Go ahead! Tell them how you killed him!

ZACHARY. You killed him too.

ROXANNE. No, no I didn't. I was out of my mind. I didn't know what I was doing!

ZACHARY. If his ghost came back it would strangle you first!

ROXANNE. Good! I wish it would. Anything would be better than dominoes every Thursday night and the same boring conversation.

ZACHARY. All right then! (*Storms out of the shop.*)

ROXANNE. (*sits still for a few moments and then begins to panic*) My God! He's really going to do it. We'll both go to prison for the rest of our lives! They'll put us in prison 'til we rot. No! No! No! (*Leaps to her feet and runs out into the street after him.*) Zack! Zachary! No! No! Don't do it! I didn't mean what I said. (*The stage is left empty for a few moments as MRS. NURDIGER sits stone still her eys burning like cold fires in their sockets. ROXANNE and ZACHARY reenter.*)

ZACHARY. I lost my nerve.

ROXANNE. I'm sorry. Oh God I'm sorry. What are we doing to ourselves? What are we doing to each other?

ZACHARY. Keep your voice down. We'll be caught. (*They crawl under the table.*)

ROXANNE. (*in a strangled whisper*) Do you think anyone heard?

ZACHARY. (*also in a hoarse whisper*) I don't know. I don't think so. I hope not.

THE ARTIFICIAL JUNGLE

(*The sound of whistling is heard approaching, they both crouch like hunted animals, frozen in terror.*)

ROXANNE. It's him—Frankie.

ZACHARY. Sometimes I think he knows. And that he's laughing at us.

ROXANNE. Don't be absurd. Why would he play with us. Please let's not add him to our nightmares.

ZACHARY. You're right. Let's pull ourselves together. Act like nothing happened. (*They rise.*)

FRANKIE. Hello, anybody home?

ROXANNE. Frankie.

FRANKIE. Domino night.

ZACHARY. Yes, domino night.

FRANKIE. You know I wouldn't let you down. And how is Mother Nurdiger doing? Ah, very well I see. In her usual chair, peaceful and contented. Surrounded by those she loves. And we all love you. Be brave. Look at her eyes. How expressive they are. She can say anything with her eyes.

ROXANNE. Here are the dominos.

FRANKIE. Won't you play for a change, Roxanne? Chester's chair looks so empty and sad. As if it missed him as much as we do.

ROXANNE. No, I couldn't. I have no mind for dominos.

ZACHARY. (*changing the subject*) Do you have any news, Frankie? Anything exciting in the field of law enforcement? As Chester used to say.

FRANKIE. Well, they caught the ones who cut up that woman into four pieces. It was the husband and another woman.

ZACHARY. I thought there were no clues?

FRANKIE. There weren't. But these two were seized with a compulsion to confess. They turned on each other. (*Mrs. Nurdiger's hand begins to rise.*) Well, will you look at that! Her hand is moving! Very good, Mother Nurdiger! Very good! Look she's making movements as though she wants to write something. She wants to communicate something.

ROXANNE. My God!

ZACHARY. Steady . . . steady.

FRANKIE. What is it, Mother Nurdiger? What is it? Look there, she's forming letters on the table. (*Watching her hand and spelling the message out loud.*) R-O-X . . . Roxanne! Yes, yes, don't bother with the rest. You've got to save your strength. A-N-D Z-A-C . . . and Zack yes I got it. Go on. A-R-E . . . are, yes, K-I . . . Oh, I know . . . kind. Roxanne and Zack are kind. She's trying to tell you how grateful she is for the way you're taking care of her. Oh, look she's trying to write some more.

ROXANNE. She's like a statue coming to life.

ZACHARY. (*taking hold of a meat cleaver*) By God, I'll cut her arm off.

FRANKIE. Come on, Mother Nurdiger what are you trying to tell us? Oh now your arm has fallen back to your side.

ROXANNE. She's turned to stone again.

ZACHARY. We're safe.

ROXANNE. For the moment.

FRANKIE. Well, shall we begin our game? I'll play for Mother Nurdiger. (*He dumps the tiles.*) Now we each take seven. (*As they draw their tiles CHESTER rises from behind the table and sits in his chair.*) Who's high?

CHESTER. Double nine. I'll be the first to go.

THE ARTIFICIAL JUNGLE 57

ZACHARY. (*Aside to ROXANNE*) He's there. He's there. Don't you see him?

ROXANNE. (*desperately aside*) Will you be quiet. There's nobody there.

FRANKIE. Zack, it's your move.

CHESTER. That's right, it's your move, Zack.

ZACHARY. It's there. It's here. It's everywhere!

FRANKIE. What? Oh that fly. (*he follows the movements and buzzing of the fly with his head and eyes*) I'll get it. (*he swats the fly*)

ROXANNE. (*screams*) No! No! Don't! Look what you did! (*Breaking down and crying.*) You killed it. You killed this innocent fly. You killed it! You killed it. (*Sobs pathetically and uncontrollably.*)

PARROT. Gawk! Hiya, Zack! What time is it? No, No, Zack that isn't funny. Ha! Ha! I can't breathe! I CAN'T BREATHE. No! No! Help me Roxanne! Roxanne! Gawk! I can't breathe.

ZACHARY. I need a drink. (*drinks*)

FRANKIE. The parrot! It almost sounds as if he were repeating . . .

ROXANNE. (*steals FRANKIE's gun*) The murder scene? Is that what you were going to say, Officer Spinelli?

PARROT. Gawk! Roxanne, help me, I can't breathe!

ROXANNE. (*fires on the parrot blowing it to bits*) And now for Mother Nurdiger.

ZACHARY. No, Roxy, don't! (*He rushes toward her, they struggle for the gun. It goes off. They both stand for a long moment looking at each other, stunned. ROXANNE slides down his body to the floor.*) Oh my God, Roxy.

ROXANNE. It's the end of the line. Everybody off. (*dies*)

FRANKIE. That was six. Give it up. I've gotta take you in.

ZACHARY. That's alright. (*Throws down the gun.*) That drink I took was malachite green, a cure for ick, poisonous to piranhas, and deadly to little men like us. I'm dying. And I look up at the stars, the thousand unseeing eyes that look back on this little speck of dust we call the world, and I ask — What was my crime compared to your indifference. I committed a senseless murder. But in its very senselessness it is in harmony with the universe which is itself senseless, and ultimately stupid. In an eon or two, who will be left to accuse me? (*dies*)

FRANKIE. Poor Chester.

(*The lights fade except for two tiny points of light on MOTHER NURDIGER's eyes.*)

THE END

Costume Plot

Zachary Slade: (Acts I, II) White tee shirt. Black jeans. Orange snakeskin jacket. Black cowboy boots. (Acts III, IV) Add a black turtleneck shirt.

Chester Nurdiger: (Acts I, IV) Light blue denim suit with a paisley print. Blue shirt with a fish print. Blue shoes. White socks. (Act II) A Tarzan costume; a white shirt with a tarantula motif; a blue nightshirt and white socks.

Frankie Spinelli: (Act I) New York City policeman's uniform; then, gray pants, matching striped shirt, gold chain around neck. (Acts II, IV) New York City policeman's uniform.

Roxanne Nurdiger: (Act I) Pink and black dress with an animal motif. Black shoes. (Act II) A green dress with an orchid motif; a black slip. (Act III) Black blouse. Black mid-length skirt. Black heels. (Act IV) Remove black skirt of Act III to reveal a black leather miniskirt.

Mother Nurdiger: (Act I) Red cotton dress. Turquoise socks. A multicolored pinafore with a fruit motif. White shoes. (Act II) A purple gown with a gold rose motif, black Keds; a green and white-striped house dress, pink slippers. (Acts III, IV) Black blouse with small white polka dots. Black skirt. Black sweater. Black shoes.

Mrs. Muncie: (Acts I, III) Black shoes. A black and white dress. A brown and gold shawl. A black hat. Three or four fox stoles.

Prop List

Act I, II

Parrot.
Piranhas.
Various pets and fish.
Hunk of meat in freezer.
Video camera.
Breakaway rock.
Large bone.
Worms.
Full ice bag.
Old sign in window.
New sign with electrical cord, wrapping paper.
Full opened and unopened wine bottles, corkscrews.
Bottle of whiskey.
Shot glass.
Set of dominoes.
Insurance policy.
Pet order form/invoice.
Meat cleaver.
Set of 5 wine glasses.
Tray of coldcuts.
Broom.
Dishrag.
Canary box.
Notepads.
Police flashlight.

At Counter
Bird toys, record, birdbath (dog dish).
Bag of proso millet, bag of birdseed.

THE ARTIFICIAL JUNGLE

Book rack and pet books (including fish book).
Sign paper.
Paper bags.
Pens and pencils.
Box with money and change, or cash register.
Bottle of malachite green and small measuring glass.

Act III, IV

Second set of dominoes.
Loaded blank gun.
Handcuffs.
Pair of panties.
More worms.
Ice pick.
Sunglasses.
Pinfeathers.
Half-eaten face mask.

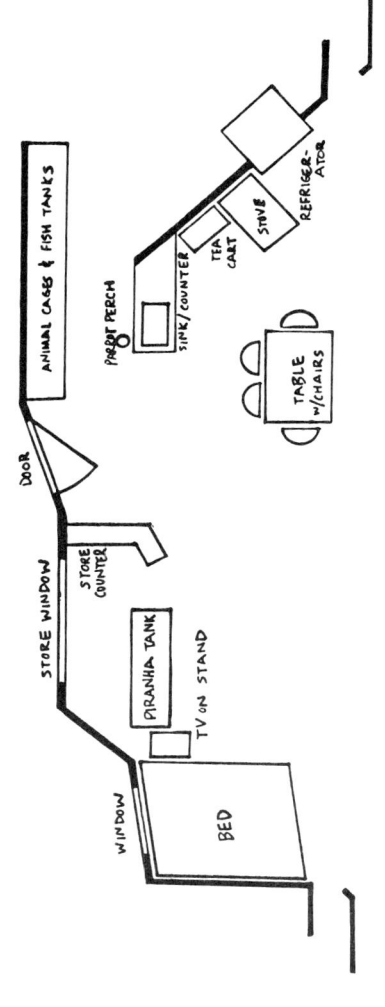

SCENE DESIGN
"THE ARTIFICIAL JUNGLE"

Other Publications for Your Interest

COMING ATTRACTIONS
(ADVANCED GROUPS—COMEDY WITH MUSIC)
By TED TALLY, music by JACK FELDMAN, lyrics by BRUCE SUSSMAN and FELDMAN

5 men, 2 women—Unit Set

Lonnie Wayne Burke has the requisite viciousness to be a media celebrity—but he lacks vision. When we meet him, he is holding only four people hostage in a laundromat. There aren't any cops much less reporters around, because they're across town where some guy is holding *50 hostages*. But, a talent agent named Manny sees possibilities in Lonnie Wayne. He devises a criminal persona for him by dressing him in a skeleton costume and sending him door-to-door, murdering people as ''The Hallowe'en Killer''. He is captured, and becomes an instant celebrity, performing on TV shows. When his fame starts to wane, he crashes the Miss America Pageant disguised as Miss Wyoming to kill Miss America on camera. However, he falls in love with her, and this eventually leads to his downfall. Lonnie ends up in the electric chair, and is fried ''live'' on prime-time TV as part of a jazzy production number! ''Fizzles with pixilated laughter.''—Time. ''I don't often burst into gales of laughter in the theatre; here, I found myself rocking with guffaws.''—New York Mag. ''Vastly entertaining.''—Newark Star-Ledger.

(Royalty, $50–$40.)

SORROWS OF STEPHEN
(ADVANCED GROUPS—COMEDY)
By PETER PARNELL

4 men, 5 women—Unit set

Stephen Hurt is a headstrong, impetuous young man—an irrepressible romantic—he's unable not to be in love. One of his models is Goethe's tragic hero, Werther, but as a contemporary New Yorker, he's adaptable. The end of an apparently undying love is followed by the birth of a grand new passion. And as he believes there's a literary precedent for all romantic possibilities justifying his choices—so with enthusiasm bordering on fickleness, he turns from Tolstoy, to Stendhal or Balzac. And Stephen's never discouraged—he can withstand rivers of rejection. (From the N.Y. Times.) And so his affairs—real and tentative—begin when his girl friend leaves him. He makes a romantic stab at a female cab driver, passes an assignation note to an unknown lady at the opera, flirts with an accessible waitress—and then has a tragic-with-comic-overtones, wild affair with his best friend's fiancée. ''Breezy and buoyant. A real romantic comedy, sophisticated and sentimental, with an ageless attitude toward the power of positive love.''—N.Y. Times.

(Royalty, $50–$40)

Other Publications for Your Interest

THE ROCKY HORROR SHOW
(MUSICAL)
Book, music and lyrics by RICHARD O'BRIEN

7 men, 3 women. Various ints. and exts.

At last! The original stage version of the cult movie that has been a "12 O'clock high " for thousands of enthusiastic movie-goers. Live, on stage, see Dr. Frank N. Furter match wits (?) with the innocent young newlyweds! Thrill to the delightfully trashy rock and roll music! "It isn't a play, it isn't a musical, it isn't a rock concert...It's a sort of glitter, rock, horror, comedy, tranvestite circus...And if you love—say, 'Sound of Music'—you will probably hate it."—WABC-TV. "*The Rocky Horror Show* is a sicko-wacko-weirdo rock concert. It keeps trying to blow your mind with loud music and perverted sexuality, but it is so simple-minded, and so completely silly, that it ends up being a lot of fun. It may get a cult following, even though there is no nudity."—NBC.
(#20049)

(Restricted. When available, Terms quoted on application—Music available on rental.) Posters Available

VAMPIRE LESBIANS OF SODOM
(ADVENTUROUS GROUPS.) FARCE
By CHARLES BUSCH

6 men, 2 women. Unit set

This truly bizarre entertainment, cut right out of the *Rocky Horror* genre, is about vamps, has nothing to do with lesbians and takes the audience from ancient Sodom to the Hollywood of the twenties, ending up somehow in present day Las Vegas. "Costumes flashier than pinball machines, outrageous lines, awful puns, sinister innocence, harmless depravity—it's all here. One can imagine a cult forming."—NY Times. "Bizarre and wonderful...If you think Boy George is a gender-bender, well, like Jolson said, you ain't seen nothing yet! Forget your genders, come on, get happy."—Broadway Mag. Published with *Sleeping Beauty*. or *Coma*. (Royalty, $50-$40.)
(#24006)

NEW OFF BROADWAY HITS
from
SAMUEL FRENCH, INC.

THE ALTO PART—BETWEEN DAYLIGHT AND BOONVILLE—BETWEEN NOW AND THEN—BIG MAGGIE—BLOOD MOON—BLUE WINDOW—CINDERS—CLARA'S PLAY—CRIMINAL MINDS—EDMOND—EXTREMITIES—FEN—THE FLIGHT OF THE EARLS—THE FREAK—GENIUSES—GREATER TUNA—HACKERS—HOMESTEADERS—THE HOUSE OF RAMON IGLESIA—HUSBANDRY—KNUCKLEBONES—LAST DAYS AT THE DIXIE GIRL CAFE—LIVING QUARTERS—LUNCH GIRLS—NURSE JANE GOES TO HAWAII—PASTORALE—QUARTERMAINE'S TERMS—ROMANCE LANGUAGE—SHIVAREE—SPLIT SECOND—TOP GIRLS—A WEEKEND NEAR MADISON—WE WON'T PAY! WE WON'T PAY!—THE WORKROOM—ZELDA

For details, consult our *Basic Catalogue of Plays.*

THE RIDICULOUS THEATRICAL COMPANY was founded in 1967 with Charles Ludlam as artistic director and playwright-in-residence. In the 20 years since its inception, the company has produced over 30 plays including Ludlam's BLUEBEARD (1970), CORN (1972), music and lyrics by Virgil Young, CAMILLE (1973), STAGE BLOOD (1975), THE VENTRILOQUIST'S WIFE (1978), THE ENCHANTED PIG (1979), REVERSE PSYCHOLOGY (1980), SECRET LIVES OF THE SEXISTS (1982), LE BOURGEOIS AVANT-GARDE (1983), GALAS (1983), THE MYSTERY OF IRMA VEP (1984), SALAMMBO (1985), and THE ARTIFICIAL JUNGLE (1986).

Both GALAS and THE MYSTERY OF IRMA VEP were cited by TIME magazine and THE NEW YORK TIMES as one of the best plays of their respective years, and IRMA VEP received the Drama Desk Award and the Obie Award for Mr. Ludlam and Everett Quinton. The company's numerous other awards include a 1981-82 Drama Desk Award for Outstanding Achievement in the Theatre, seven additional Obie Awards, and BITEF and Drama-Logue awards. In 1986, Mr. Ludlam won the Rosamund Gilder Award for distinguished achievement in the theatre, and in 1987 he received a Village Voice Obie Award for distinguished achievement.

THE RIDICULOUS THEATRICAL COMPANY has toured extensively in the U.S., Canada and throughout Europe.

Charles Ludlam died May 28, 1987 at the age of 44.

ISBN 0-573-69072-3   #3932

LIBRARY OF DAVIDSON COLLEGE

Books on regular loan may be checked out for **two weeks**. Books must be presented at the Circulation Desk in order to be renewed.

A fine is charged after date due.

Special books are subject to special regulations at the discretion of the library staff.

APR 0 8 1993			
MAY 0 8 1993			